Introduction

Finally a VEGAN-friendly cookbook for Harry Potter fans! T*he Unofficial Harry Potter Cookbook for Vegans* is an amazing collection of delicious vegan recipes, all inspired by the wondrous and magical Wizarding World of Harry Potter.

This book contains absolutely brilliant dishes taken straight out of the Potter series, with a delicious vegan twist that everyone, even your carnivourius friends can enjoy!

Have you ever wondered what Mrs. Weasley's cornish pasties taste like? Have you ever wanted to experience the joys of a creamy cold Knickerbocker treat? You'll find all of that in this book as well as *exclusive* recipes unique to us, like Quidditch Game Day Nachos!

With a dash of creativity, a sprinkle of fun and a light dusting of magic, this book will help you whip up everything, from Mrs. Weasley approved breakfasts, to lunches and appetizers, to Hogwarts dinners and tasty desserts!

This book makes a wonderful gift for all the vegan, vegetarian or plant-based Harry Potter fans in your life. But meat lovers need not shy away. Taste will always be a priority in our books, so you don't want to miss all the goodness between these pages. Need I say more? Come in and explore the world of Harry Potter in a whole new, delectable way!

TABLE OF CONTENTS

Breakfast

Bangers and Mash

In the Order of the Phoenix, Harry Potter was enjoying this traditional British dish for breakfast.

Explanation: A classic and comforting english breakfast made of sausages and mashed potatoes with warm gravy poured on top.

Prep: 20 mins Cook: 30 mins Serves: 4

Materials:

- Small pot
- Medium skillet
- Large saucepan
- Potato masher

Ingredients:

- 8 vegan sausages of choice

For mash:

- 1 lb potatoes
- 1 cup plant milk
- 2 tbsp vegan butter
- 2 tsp salt
- ½ tsp pepper
- 1 tsp garlic powder

For gravy

- 1 large yellow onion chopped
- 2 garlic cloves minced
- 250 g (8oz) white button mushrooms halved
- 2 medium tomatoes chopped
- 100 g (3.5 oz) walnuts
- 1 tsp sage powder
- 1 tsp paprika
- 2 tsp salt
- 1 tsp pepper
- 2 cups vegetable stock

Instructions:

- Thaw the sausages if frozen
- Place the walnuts in a food processor, chop until texture resembles that of fine flour.
- Peel the potatoes and cut roughly, then place in a pot and cover with cold water, add 1 tbsp salt and place over high heat. Once the water comes to a boil, boil the potatoes for 15 mins or until tender and cooked through.
- Drain the water out and pour in the milk and butter directly into the pot with the potatoes, make sure it is off the heat, then mash together with a potato masher until smooth, then add the salt, pepper and garlic powder. Taste and adjust seasoning as desired. Set aside.
- To prepare the gravy, in a saucepan, pour a couple of tablespoons of oil and put the onions in then sautee for 5 mins or until the onions are translucent.
- Add the garlic and mushrooms and saute for another 5 mins, then add the tomatoes, saute for another 8-10 minutes, until the tomatoes and mushrooms have released their liquid,
- Add the vegetable stock, walnut flour and seasoning. Simmer on medium low heat for 15 minutes. Set aside to cool
- After the gravy mixture has cooled, place in a food processor and puree until very smooth.
- Strain the gravy into a sauce pot, taste for seasoning and adjust as needed, reheat for serving
- The last step will be adding 2 tbsp of olive oil to a skillet over high heat, then place the sausages in there, grilling them 2-3 minutes on each side, until a nice brown color develops.

How to serve:

- Place a large spoonful or 2 of the mash in the middle of the plate, over that 2 sausages. Then about a ladleful of the gravy over the top.

Chef's tip:

- Garnish with chopped parsley to add a little color and extra flavor to the dish.

Breakfast Porridge

Porridge is a staple breakfast food in England, and it's not hard to imagine this dish regularly appearing at Breakfast in the Great Hall each day. Perfect for those crisp winter mornings...

Explanation: It is a warm cereal dish made by boiling grain with water or milk. Experiment with different milks for interesting, and unique versions each time you make it!

Prep: 10 mins Cook: 5 mins Serves: 2

Materials:

- Small sauce pot

Ingredients:

- 1 cup rolled oats (instant oats also works)
- 2 ½ cups plant milk
- 1 tbsp agave
- 1 tsp salt
- ½ tsp ground cinnamon
- ¼ tsp ground nutmeg

Toppings (optional)

- 2 bananas sliced
- Fresh berries
- ¼ cup Almond slices
- 2 tbsp raisins

Instructions:

- Place the oats, milk and agave in a small sauce pot over medium heat.
- After about 2 mins, add in the salt, cinnamon and nutmeg. Over a very low simmer, let the oats cook for about 5 mins until most of the liquid is absorbed. Be sure to stir constantly to prevent the bottom from sticking and burning.

How to serve:

- Pour your porridge into separate bowls and get creative with your toppings of choice from fruits, to nuts to whatever else you like.

Chef's tips:

- Add a tbsp of cocoa powder to oats while they are cooking to for a rich, chocolatey flavor. If you are not allergic, top with a tsp of peanut butter.

Breakfast Tofu Scramble

Everyone loves a nice warm plate of scrambled eggs in the morning.,the Wizards and Witches of Hogwarts being no exception. Decorate your tofu scrambled eggs however you like, and pair with fruit and toast for a complete breakfast.

Explanation: spiced tofu scramble that resembles scrambled eggs makes a great and tasty breakfast dish.

Prep time: 15 mins Cook time: 20 mins Serves: 2

Materials:
- Skillet

Ingredients:
- 1 package firm tofu
- ½ tsp salt
- ½ tsp pepper
- ½ tsp turmeric powder
- ¼ tsp mustard powder
- ¼ tsp garlic powder
- ¼ tsp onion powder
- ¼ tsp cumin

- ⅛ tsp cayenne pepper (optional)
- 1 tbsp coconut oil

Instructions:

- In a medium sized bowl, crumble the tofu using a fork to an almost mash-like consistency. .
- Heat the oil in the skillet, then add the tofu, toss around the skillet for about a minute then add the spices.
- Add all the spices at once and stir well to incorporate everything into the tofu.
- Taste and adjust salt and pepper as desired

How to serve:

- You can serve this family style on a platter so guests can help themselves
- Or you can serve it immediately onto the guests plates or onto their toast

Chef's tips:

- Add some green into the mix such as cilantro or green onion to give it a bright color and extra flavor.
- Add your favorite hot sauce to spice it up a bit if you like spicy food!

Butterbeer Pancakes

What we imagine would be on the breakfast menu at the Three Broomsticks.

Explanation: A classic fluffy breakfast with a magical twist that is quick and easy to make.

Prep time: 15 mins Cook time: 20 mins Serves: 4

Materials needed:

- Medium skillet
- Small sauce pot

Ingredients:

For the pancakes:

- 1 cup flour
- 2 tbsp sugar
- 1 tbsp baking powder
- ½ tsp salt
- 1 cup plant milk
- 1 tsp vanilla
- 1 tbsp coconut oil

For Serving:

- ⅓ cup vegan butter

- ⅔ cup cane sugar (brown sugar also works)
- ½ cup coconut cream
- 1 tsp vanilla
- 1 tsp salt

Instructions:

- In a bowl, combine together the dry ingredients, the flour, sugar, baking powder and salt. Mix well.
- In a separate bowl, combine together the wet ingredients, the plant milk, coconut oil and vanilla.
- Pour the wet ingredients into the dry ingredients and whisk well to combine. Let the batter sit for 5-10 mins then whisk once more to ensure that there are no lumps and that the batter is smooth.
- In a sauce pot, melt the vegan butter, then add the sugar and salt to it, stir well until the sugar has dissolved.
- Over medium heat, continue to stir the sauce until it starts to bubble, then add the vanilla and the coconut cream, carefully because it may splatter.
- Bring the heat up to medium-high and boil the sauce for about 8-10 minutes, or until it has reached a dark amber color. Do not over cook, or the sauce will start to harden when cooled.
- In a medium skillet, brush the bottom with oil and add ⅓ cup of the pancake batter. Cook on one side for 3-4 minutes, when the pancake starts to brown, then flip it and cook for another 2 minutes.

How to serve:

- Stack on each plate 3 pancakes, and drizzle the sauce on top.

Chef's tips:

- Sprinkle some powdered sugar on top of the sauce on the pancakes sor added visual appeal and sweetness
- If you like a less sweetened sauce, then instead of the 1 tsp of salt, add 1 tbsp to create this sweet and salty sauce.

Salads & Soups

House Hufflepuff Butternut Squash Soup

The Hufflepuff Common Rooms are located in the basement, next to the kitchens. One would imagine it gets pretty chilly down there. Hence, what better way to warm up than with a rich, creamy and even sweet butternut soup.

Explanation: Pureed butternut with a delicious twist

Prep time: 15 mins Cook time: 45 mins Serves: 6

Materials:
- Medium pot
- Blender

Ingredients:
- 1 large butternut squash (3 - 4lbs)
- 1 large onion
- 3 garlic cloves peeled and diced
- 13.5-oz. can unsweetened coconut milk, divided
- 2 tbsp. extra virgin olive oil
- 1 piece of fresh ginger, chopped (approx. 2 inches)

- ¼ tsp. Sea salt
- 1 lime
- ½ cup unsweetened coconut flakes
- ¼ tsp. crushed red pepper flakes
- A small handful of cilantro, with stems

Instructions:

- Cut and Peel squash into smaller pieces (you may wish to use gloves to protect them from the sometimes skin irritating juices) This soup is well-worth the effort, trust us!

- Chop the remaining ingredients, don't worry too much about the sizes since you will be blending everything. Ginger is best grated however.

- Heat 2 tbsp of oil in a saucepan over medium and add onions, ginger, garlic, pepper flakes, salt. Stir with wooden spoon until they are fragrant and translucent and soft, 5-7 minutes.

Add squash and coat everything with 3 cups of water, or enough to submerge the squash. Add the coconut milk, and stir to combine. Raise heat to a boil.

Once it boils, reduce heat to medium and allow to simmer. Stir until the veggies are very tender,. Approx. 12–14 minutes.

Prep your garnishes by placing unsweetened coconut flakes on a baking tray and browning them in the oven. (Be sure to watch them so they do not burn!) Cut and squeeze the juice of 1 lime. (You can use ½ – 1 lime's worth of juice in your soup, it's up to you.) If you have extra limes you can halve them for garnishes on the soup bowls.

- Use ladel to fill blender halfway with broth and veggies (no more than half at a time should be blended to avoid spillage) IMPORTANT: When securing your blender lid, make sure there is a vent for steam to escape. (Most blenders have a small cover on the very top of the lid, remove this while blending to avoid blender lid from shooting off and a messy kitchen!

How to serve: Ladel soup in bowls, swirl in any extra reserves of coconut milk, and top with coconut flakes, cilantro and a wedge of lime at the side if you fancy.

Chef's tip: Top with pumpkin spice. Also this recipe can be made with apples, and/or carrots along with the squash.

Hagrid's Forest Stew

Hagrid's hut is located at the edge of the forbidden forest, it would make sense that he would go foraging for ingredients to make a great stew in his cauldron over the fire in the warmth and comfort of his own home.

Explanation: A chunky and hearty vegan stew that's perfect for a winter evening.

Prep time: 20 mins Cook time: 40 mins Serves: 6

Materials:

- Large soup pot

Ingredients:

- 2 large onions, chopped
- 2 garlic cloves, chopped
- 4 celery stalks, chopped
- 1 yellow bell pepper, chopped
- 1 red bell pepper, chopped
- 1 medium potato, peeled and chopped
- 1 large carrot, peeled and chopped
- 1 medium sweet potato, peeled and chopped
- 1 cup baby portobello mushrooms, sliced in half, smaller if needed
- 4 cups vegetable stock

- 1 tsp garlic powder
- 1 tsp onion powder
- 1 tsp ground sage
- 1 tsp ground basil
- 1 tsp dried thyme
- 1 tsp paprika
- 1 tsp pepper
- Salt to taste

Instructions:

- Before cooking, make sure all the vegetables are cut into similar sizes to ensure even cooking of everything. The mushrooms, however, can be slightly larger.
- Pour the vegetable stock into the large pot, then place all the vegetables inside. Over medium high heat, bring the stew to a simmer.
- After about 10 mins of simmering, add all the spices into the soup, continue to simmer for another 30 minutes. Taste and adjust the salt and pepper per your desired taste.
- All the vegetables should be perfectly tender and cooked through, the stew should be chunky, and almost half the liquid should cook out.

How to serve:

- Serve family style in a large serving soup bowl for everyone to enjoy.

Chef's tips:

- Having slices of warm toasted bread with this stew would make a complete meal.
- If you want, you could drizzle some vegan basil pesto on top of the stew once served in individual bowls.

Kreacher's French Onion Soup

In the Deathly Hallows, Kreacher has become much better at cooking and makes the trio a delicious French Onion Soup

Explanation: It is a classical french dish of caramelized onions and a rich broth.

Prep time: 20 mins Cook time: 1 hr Serves: 2

Materials:

- Medium pot
- Small baking tray

Ingredients:

For the soup

- 1 tbsp vegan butter
- 4 medium yellow onions
- 1 tsp sugar (cane sugar or agave)
- 1 tbsp almond flour
- 2.5 cups vegetable stock
- ¼ cup red wine

- 1 bay leaf
- 1 tsp thyme (dried of fresh)
- Salt
- Pepper

For croutons

- 2 tbsp vegan butter, room temperature
- 2-4 slices of baguette bread, ½ in thick
- ¼ cup vegan parmesan cheese

Instructions:

- Preheat the oven to 350 F.
- Peel the onions, cut in half then slice thinly, place in a bowl and set aside.
- Melt the vegan butter in the pot over medium-high heat, then add the onions. Saute the onions for 10 mins until translucent, then turn the heat down to medium-low and continue to caramelize for another 15 mins.
- Then add the sugar, salt, pepper and thyme and continue to caramelize for another 15 mins. It should have a very deep golden brown color.
- Deglaze with the red wine. Stir until half of the wine is cooked out, then add the flour and cook for about 2-3 minutes. Add the stock and stir well to make sure there are no clumps, and then simmer on low for 15-20 minutes.
- Taste for seasoning and adjust to your taste, then turn the heat to low and simmer for another 15-20 minutes.
- While the soup is cooking, make the croutons. Butter both sides of the baguette slices and place on the baking tray, sprinkle the cheese on top then bake for 5 minutes.

How to serve:

- Serve your delicious soup into separate bowls alongside your crunchy and cheesy croutons.

Chef's tips:

- Make sure to use yellow onions because they will give you the consistency and flavor you are looking for.
- For the vegan cheese, something similar to parmesan works best, try brands like Parma! Or Nooch It!

Gillyweed Salad

Trying to make gillyweed appetizing after Harry made it very clear that it isn't was a challenge. But you will definitely love this take on it.

Explanation: A refreshing salad made using wakame, a type of seaweed that is commonly used in japanese cuisine to represent gillyweed.

Prep time: 10 mins Cook time: 5 mins Serves: 4

Ingredients:

- 15 g (0.5 oz) dried wakame
- 2 tsp miso paste
- 1 tbsp apple cider vinegar
- 1 tbsp soy sauce
- 2 tsp agave
- 1 tbsp sesame seeds.

Instructions:

- Place the wakame in a bowl and pour boiling water over it to soften. Let it sit for 5 mins then drain the water out and set aside in a bowl to cool slightly.
- While cooling, mix together the miso, soy sauce, apple vinegar, agave and sesame seeds in a small bowl, and pour over the wakame. Give it a good mix until everything is well incorporated.

How to serve:

- Sprinkle some sesame seeds on top and enjoy!

Chef's tip:

- Some people's palates are not very adventurous, and may not love the idea of eating seaweed. Just substitute the seaweed with lettuce of choice.

Luna Lovegood's Summer Salad

The Lovegood's front yard is a sight to behold with all its fantastically delicious homegrown fruits and vegetables. It would be quite simple to imagine them enjoying gourmet salads like this on the regular.

Explanation: A quick, simple, and healthy salad to have at summer BBQs

Prep time: 30 mins Cook time: - Serves: 4

Materials needed:

- Mandolin slicer
- bowl

Ingredients:

- 10 small red radishes (stem and root trimmed)
- 20 English cucumbers
- 2 garlic cloves, minced
- 1 small red onion
- ½ cup olive oil
- 2 tbsp white vinegar (or apple if you prefer)
- 1 tsp salt
- ½ tsp pepper
- ½ tbsp dill
- 1 tsp agave

Instructions:

- Using the mandolin, slice thinly the radishes, cucumber, and onion. Place them in a bowl with the dill
- Make the dressing by combining the olive oil, vinegar, garlic, salt, and pepper. Mix well together until thickened.

How to serve:

- The sliced vegetables and dressing should be separate until serving time.
- This salad is best when refrigerated.

Chef's tips:

- You can add any other local summer vegetables to the salad such as carrots, fennel, bell peppers, beetroot and tomatoes.

Appetizers & Sides

House Gryffindor Buffalo Cauliflower Wings

This is a dish that is very commonly associated with game days, so naturally any vegan Gryffindor would love to enjoy this tasty and messy dish after a long day of quidditch.

Explanation: Instead of chicken wings, we use baked cauliflower covered in sauce

Prep time: 15 mins Cook time: 20 mins Serves: 4

Materials:

- Medium saucepan
- Oven tray

Ingredients:

- 1 head of cauliflower
- ½ plant milk
- 1 cup flour
- 2 tsp garlic powder
- 1 tsp paprika
- 1 tsp pepper
- 1 tsp cumin
- 1 tsp salt
- ½ cup sriracha
- 1 tbsp vegan butter
-

Instructions:

- Preheat the oven to 375 F. Line the baking tray with tin foil. Drizzle oil on the foil.
- Cut the cauliflower head into bite sized florets, you should end up with about 4 cups of florets.
- In a bowl combine the flour, plant milk and spices, mix well until smooth and no lumps appear, should resemble pancake batter. Pour the cauliflower into the batter, shake the excess batter off, then lay them out on the baking tray making sure they don't touch.
- Bake for 20 mins, until they are golden brown. Flip the cauliflower halfway through to ensure even cooking.
- While the cauliflower is baking, in a small sauce pot, pour the sriracha sauce along with the butter. Stir to melt the butter over medium-low heat. When the butter has melted and incorporated, remove and set aside
- Remove the cauliflower while still hot and place in a large bowl. Pour over the sauce and toss to evenly coat everything.

How to serve:

- Serve on a large platter so guests can easily enjoy.

Chef's tips:

- If you don't want it spicy, substitute the sriracha with vegan BBQ sauce.

Quidditch Game Day Nachoes

Who cares if it's not in the books? Everyone loves nachoes! After the winning team retreats to their dorms, still excited and pumped about the game, a large array of food must surely await them! These vegan nachoes really hit the spot! Washh it down with a vegan *Butterbeer* or a glass of Fire Whisky from our *Harry Potter Cocktails and Mocktails* book.

Explanation: Vegan loaded nachoes

Prep time: 15 mins Cook time: 15 mins Serves: Depends if you feel like sharing

Materials:

- baking trays
- parchment papers
- small sauce pans (2)

Ingredients:

- 8 cups of restaurant-style tortilla chips (or any of your choice)
- 1 cup of guacamole (more if you choose)
- 115-ounce can of black beans (re-fried is awesome)
- Fresh jalapenos
- Diced red onion
- Black olives
- Vegan queso
- Chunky salsa (1 cup approx)
- Cilantro (optional)

- Hot sauce of your choice (optional)
- Vegan ground beef or similar plant-based meat (optional but is amazing with taco seasoning)

Instructions:

- Preheat the oven to 350 F. Line the 2 baking trays with parchment paper.
- Prepare your guacamole
- Warm your queso in a small saucepan
- Heat up beans in another pan with spices like cumin, garlic powder and chili powder
- Take your oven-safe baking sheet or tray and pour some chips onto it, a layer of toppings (we suggest beans first, queso, salsa, guac, onions, jalapenos, cilantro and hot sauce)
- Repeat until all the chips are on the tray/sheet
- Place in oven for 5-10 minutes, or until warm/hot

How to serve:

- Serve right away while hot! And wash it down with a delicious drink

Chef's tips:

- Guacamole is best made at home. Use ripe avocadoes (1 large or 2 small), cut and smash, add ¼ sea salt, and lime juice (play with porportions to your liking)

- Vegan queso can be purchased in stores, including online stores, even on Amazon

- *When making nachoes layer the toppings throughout the chips so you get yummy toppings with every bite, instead of just on top of the chips.

Cornish Pasties

" 'It's alright' he (Ron) said, helping himself to a cornish pasty...."
- Harry Potter and the Goblet of Fire

Explanation: It is a stuffed pastry that is baked. It is usually a savory dish, similar to a calzone or an empanada.

Prep time: 1 hr Cook time: 1 hr Serves: 5

Materials:
- Baking tray
- Food processor

Ingredients:
For the filling
- 500 g (1 lb) minced vegan beef
- 1 medium turnip, diced small
- 1 large onion, diced small
- 1 medium potato, diced small
- ¼ cup worcestershire sauce
- ½ cup tomato sauce
- Salt
- Pepper

For the pastry
- 3 ½ cup flour
- 225 g (½ lb) vegan butter, cold
- 1 tsp salt
- ¼ cup coconut oil
- ¼ cup ice water

Instructions:

- Chop the vegetables, then place in a bowl and mix with the vegan meat, worcestershire and tomato sauce and season with salt and pepper. Set aside to marinade.
- In a food processor, add the flour, butter, and salt. Pulse a few times until the dough starts forming and coming together. Turn out onto a floured surface and knead together until a smooth but firm dough forms. Wrap with plastic and refrigerate for 30 minutes.
- Preheat the oven to 350 F. Line the baking tray with baking paper.
- Roll out the dough onto a floured surface until ¼ in thick. Cut out 5 in circles from the dough. If you have a lot of scraps, knead and roll out the dough again, then cut out more circles.
- Scoop a few tbsp of the filling into the center of the dough, brush the sides of the dough circle with water, and fold over the dough to form a “D” shape. Pinch and crimp the curved side of the pasty to make sure nothing comes out, then make 2-3 small incisions at the top of the pasty to allow steam to escape when needed. Brush the top with coconut oil.
- Bake in the oven for 45 mins to 1 hr or until golden brown on the outside.

How to serve:

- Allow the pasties to cool for about 10-15 mins before enjoying
- Serve them on a large platter for guests to grab easily.

Chef’s tips:

- If you have access to ready made vegan dough, it will cut the prep time greatly.
- Add any fresh herbs and spices you like to the filling to add flavor.

Yorkshire Pudding

"'Oh c'mon er-my-knee' said Ron, accidentally spraying Harry with bits of yorkshire pudding."
- Harry Potter and the Goblet of Fire

Explanation: A traditional bread like side dish that is commonly served at a roast to accompany the main dishes.

Prep time: 15 mins Cook time: 30 mins Serves: 8

Materials:
- Muffin tin
- Jug

Ingredients:
- 1 ⅓ cup flour
- 2 ¼ tsp baking powder
- ¼ tsp salt
- ½ tsp dijon mustard
- 1 tsp apple cider vinegar
- ⅓ cup aquafaba
- 1 ½ cup water
- Vegetable or coconut oil as needed

Instructions:
- Preheat the oven to 425 F
- Mix your dry ingredients in a bowl. The flour, salt and baking powder.
- In a separate bowl, mix together the mustard, vinegar, aquafaba and water, whisk together until well combined.

- Pour the wet ingredients over the dry ingredients and whisk well together until smooth and well incorporated. Rest the batter for 10 mins then whisk again to make sure there are no lumps. Pour into a jug for easy portioning.
- Add 1-2 tbsp of oil into the bottom of each well in the muffin tray, place in the oven for 10 mins, you should see smoke start to rise from the oil in the wells.
- Take the pan out and carefully pour the batter into each well, fill until about ½ an inch from the top. Move quickly and carefully, the trick is that the oil has to be very hot in order for this recipe to work.
- Place back in the oven and bake for 30-40 mins until golden brown and crispy. Make sure not to open the oven too early in order to make sure you get the desired shape of the puddings.

How to serve:

- Serve on a platter as a side dish.
- Should be served hot.

Chef's tips:

- Aquafaba is the liquid from a can of chickpeas
- This side dish would go really well with a main dish that has a sauce component.

Sandwiches

House Ravenclaw Beet and Pinenut Flatbread

A delicious flatbread inspired by the brilliant and studious Ravenclaw House. A healthy, and easy meal that perfectly fits the busy schedule of any Ravenclaw. Enjoy whenever you crave guilt-free comfort food, without the fuss.

Explanation: A delicious and unique flatbread, with beets, cheese and pinenuts.

Prep time: 5 Cook Time: 30 Serves: 1 person or more if you wish to make it an appetizer

Materials:

- Knife

- Sauce pan

- Oven tray

Ingredients:

- 1 large nann bread

- 2 tbsp basil pesto

- 1 tbsp balsamic vinegar

- 2 small beets boiled, then thinly sliced

- 1/4 cup broccolini florets

- 2 tbsp pine nuts toasted

- 1/4 cup mozzarella cheese vegan, shredded

Instructions:

- Fill up a saucepan with water (half way), and bring to a boil over high heat.

- Cut beets in half, boil for 15-20 mins, or until a knife can be easily inserted in the side. Then set aside to cool.

- Next preheat oven to 350° F.

- Spread pesto over the flatbread, making sure to leave approx. 1/2 inch of edge uncovered, for the crust.

- Add a thin layer thinly sliced beets, then add broccolini.

- Sprinkle an even layer of cheese over the bread

- Top it off with pine nuts for a crunchy finish

- Place in oven, then cook for 10-15 minutes, or until bottom of the naan bread is golden brown.

- Drizzle your balsamic over the flatbread. Enjoy!

Chef's tips:

- Cut the beets in half or quarters, so they can cook faster.

Bottomless Sandwich Plate

When Harry is over at the Weasley's house, a Bottomless plate of sandwiches appears before them. No matter how many sandwiches they eat, the plate just magically refills itself again.

Explanation: A large platter full of 3 types of vegan sandwiches, cucumber, tempeh and BLT (bacon, lettuce and tomato)

Prep time: 30 mins Cook time: 10 mins Serves: 6

Materials:
- Large platter for serving
- Small pan

Ingredients
- 36 slices of toast (your toast of choice)

For the cucumber sandwiches
- 2-3 English cucumbers, sliced thin
- ½ cup vegan cream cheese

For the tempeh sandwiches
- 300 g (10.5 oz) Tempeh, ¼ in slices
- 1 package baby arugula leaves
- ½ cup vegan butter, room temperature
- ½ cup water
- 3 tbsp soy sauce
- 2 tbsp apple cider vinegar
- 2 tbsp olive oil
- 1 tsp garlic powder
- 1 tsp paprika

- 1 tsp pepper
- ½ tsp salt

For the BLT sandwiches

- ½ cup vegan mayonnaise
- ¼ cup mustard
- 1-2 head of lettuce leaves
- 3 medium tomatoes, sliced thin
- 1 package Vegan bacon

Instructions:

For the Cucumber sandwiches

- On 12 slices of toast, spread the vegan cheese to a thin layer on one side of each slice. Arrange the cucumber slices on 6 of the toasts, then use the other 6 to sandwich the cucumber.

For the Tempeh Sandwiches

- In a large bowl, combine the water, soy sauce, apple vinegar, olive oil, garlic powder, paprika, salt and pepper and mix well to combine. Place the Tempeh slices in the marinade, and place in the fridge for at least 1 hr.
- Remove Tempeh from marinade and drain the tempeh well. Place a pan over medium-high heat with 1 tbsp of olive oil, then sear the marinated tempeh on both sides for about 2 mins a side, until a nice golden color develops.
- On 12 slices of toast, spread a thin layer of the vegan butter. Then on 6 of the buttered slices, place a nice handful of the arugula leaves, and top with 3-4 slices of the marinated and seared Tempeh.Sandwich the last slice of toast on top.

For the BLT sandwiches

- Oven a medium high heat, place a pan with 1 tbsp of oil and sear the vegan bacon on both sides until starting to crisp, about a minute or two each side. Take out and place on paper towels to remove any extra grease.
- On 6 slices of toast, spread a thin layer of the vegan mayo, and on the other 6 slices, spread a thin layer of the mustard.
- Start assembling the sandwich, mayo toast on the bottom, then the lettuce, 3-4 slices of tomato, 3-4 slices of crispy bacon, then the mustard toast on top.

How to serve:

- Serve on a large platter, feel free to mix and match the sandwiches they do not have to be in order of anything.
- Make sure not to present all the sandwiches at once so that every time the plate is emptied, refill it with more sandwiches, giving the illusion of a bottomless sandwich plate.

Chef's tips:

- Use a mandolin to thinly slice the cucumbers, it will ensure even sizes.
- Feel free to add any type of sandwiches you like to the mix, maybe have a peanut butter and jelly sandwich.

Mrs. Weasley's Smoked Tempeh Bacon Sandwich: Harry Potter

"After a quick half a dozen bacon sandwiches each. They pulled on their coats…" - Harry Potter and the Chamber of Secrets

Explanation: Mrs. Weasley is quite the wonderful mother and cook, and this "bacon" sandwich would be a hit at her breakfast table. Just make sure to get there before Fred and George finish it all off!

Prep time: 10 mins Cook time: 10 mins Serves: 2

Materials needed:
- Pan

Ingredients:
- 8 slices of smoked tempeh (for "candied bacon" drizzle maple syrup on these bad boys, just be sure to watch so they don't burn)
- 4 slices of your favorite bread
- Vegan butter (4 tbsp) or vegan mayo
- Oil for frying (2 tsp)

Instructions:
- Fry the bacon in the pan in the oil for 2 mins each side, until crispy. Then set aside.

- Butter both sides of the 4 slices of bread. Sandwich every 4 slices of bacon in between 2 slices of bread.
- Toast the outside of the bread over medium heat on the pan until golden brown. About a minute on each side.

How to serve:

- Slice the sandwiches in half to reveal the crispy bacon in the middle.

Chef's tips:

- You can add tomatoes, lettuce and avocadoes to the sandwich before frying to add more flavors and textures.

Curried Pumpkin Burger

A deliciously flavorful burger that has all the first week of Wizarding school in the Fall vibes.

Explanation: This is a homemade vegan burger with an indian twist.

Prep time: 15 mins Cook time: 40 mins Serves: 8

Materials needed:

- Large ice cream scoop
- Baking tray
- 2 bowls
- Potato masher

Ingredients:

- 1 cup pumpkin puree
- 1 cup rolled oats
- 1 can white beans (rinsed well)
- 2 tbsp ground flax seeds
- ¼ cup hot water
- 2 tbsp nutritional yeast
- 1 tsp garam masala
- ½ tsp garlic powder
- ½ tsp ginger powder
- ½ tsp turmeric powder
- ½ tsp cumin powder
- ¼ tsp cardamom powder
- ¼ tsp onion powder
- 1 tsp salt
- ½ tsp pepper
- ¼ tsp cayenne pepper (optional)

To serve:

- 8 burger buns
- 8-10 leaves of lettuce
- 16 slices of tomato
- Mustard
- Sliced pickles (optional)

Instructions:

- Preheat the oven to 375°F
- Grease a baking tray.
- Add flax seeds to hot water, let sit for 10 mins.
- Mash the beans well with a potato masher, and place in a bowl. Add the pumpkin puree, oats, yeast, garam masala, garlic, ginger, turmeric, cumin, cardamom, onion, salt, pepper and cayenne along with the flax seed mixture. Mix well to incorporate all of the ingredients.
- Using the ice cream scoop, divide the mixture into 8 "patties" and place on the baking tray. Press down the top of the patties with a spoon. (dip the spoon in water first to prevent sticking)
- Place in the oven and bake for 20 mins, take out the tray and flip the patties over, return the tray to the oven for another 20 mins.
- Burger Assembly Instructions? Wala fakes?

How to serve:

- Make sure to allow the patties to cool before assembly. Assemble the burger as you wish, in whichever order you prefer.

Chef's tips:

- Serve with sweet potato fries, and vegan mild cheese

Paddington Burgers

You can never go wrong at any lunch or dinner with a build your own burger station.

Explanation: A vegan twist on a classic dish.

Prep time: 20 mins Cook time: 15 mins Serves: 4

Materials needed:
- Large skillet

Ingredients:
For the patties
- 1 lb vegan ground meat (beyond meat works great)
- 1 tsp garlic powder
- 1 tsp onion powder
- 1 tsp dried oregano
- 1 tbsp tomato paste
- 1 tbsp vegetable oil

For the burger:
- 4 burger buns
- 1 cup shredded lettuce
- 1 small thinly sliced red onion
- 2 tomatoes sliced
- 1 pickle sliced (optional)

Instructions:
- Mix the vegan meat, garlic powder, onion powder, ogano, and tomato paste well. Divide the mixture into 4 patties.
- Pour 1 tbsp oil into the large skillet and place it over medium-high heat. Place the patties in the skillet and cook for 2 mins on each side.

- Once the patties are done, you are ready to serve.
- Burger assembly instructions below

How to serve:

- Serve each patty in a bun, place every topping (lettuce, onions, tomatoes, and pickles) in small plates to the side so guests can help themselves and enjoy building their own burgers.

Chef's tips:

- Classic condiments like ketchup, mustard, and mayonnaise could also be great additions to the table.

Fish Finger Sandwiches

"I told you to stay away from those fish finger sandwiches."

- Harry Potter and the Cursed Child

Explanation of dish: A quick, easy dish for a light and traditional midday lunch.

Prep time: 15 minutes / Cook time: 10 minutes / Serving size: 2 Sandwiches

Materials needed:

- Frying pan

Ingredients Needed:

For Fish Fingers:

- 2 blocks of firm tofu
- ½ Cup ap. flour
- 1/4 cup plant milk
- 2 tbsp. soy sauce
- 2 tbsp. lemon juice
- 1 cup bread crumbs

- 1 tsp. pepper

For Sandwich:

- 6 Fish Fingers
- 4 slices of white bread or bread of choice
- 4 lettuce leaves, washed
- 2 tbsp. of vegan mayo
- 1 tbsp. of vegan butter

Instructions:

- Preheat the oven to 375 F.
- Slice tofu into 6 equal strips and coat well with flour.
- In a shallow bowl, whisk plant milk, soy sauce, and lemon juice. In another shallow bowl, combine bread crumbs and pepper.
- Gently dip floured tofu in soy milk mixture, then coat all sides well in bread crumbs.
- Pan-fry on both sides in a bit of oil for 2-3 minutes or until golden brown.
- When done frying, place fish sticks on paper towels to drain the oil. Set aside.
- Get 2 slices of bread and butter each slice.
- Spread 1 tbsp. of mayo on a buttered slice of bread.
- Place a lettuce leaf on top of mayo and line 3 fish fingers side by side on top of the lettuce.
- Place another lettuce leaf on top of the lined fish fingers then top with the other slice of bread.
- Repeat steps 7-10 for the second sandwich.

How to Serve:

- Cut each sandwich in half and serve.

Chef tips

- Best served with a side of pickles and vegan tartar sauce on the side

Main Courses

Cho's Chinese Fireballs

Easy to prepare and a clever way to make your guests serve themselves. These vegan meatballs were inspired by Cho Chang and the rich and delicious, hot and sweet, flavors in Chinese cuisine. Experiment with various sauces/dips to accompany this finger food. If you cant handle spice, you may want to skip this one...

Explanation: Small vegan meatballs with a sweet and spicy dipping sauce.

Prep time: 30 mins Cook time: 20 mins Serves: 5

Materials needed:
- Small sauce pot
- Baking tray

Ingredients:

For the meatballs
- 1 lb ground beyond meat (or similar)
- ½ cup bread crumbs
- 1 tsp garlic powder
- 1 tsp onion powder
- 1 ½ tsp salt
- 1 tsp pepper

For the dipping sauce:

- ½ cup bbq sauce
- ½ cup raspberry jam
- 2 tbsp mustard (dijon preferably)
- 2 tsp worcestershire sauce
- 2 tbsp sriracha
- 1 tsp salt
- 1 tsp pepper
- liquid smoke

Instructions:

- Preheat the oven to 400 F, and grease the baking tray well.
- In a large bowl mix together all the ingredients for the meatballs very well until all the breadcrumbs and spices are well incorporated.
- Using a tablespoon, scoop a portion of the meatball mixture and proceed to roll them out into small spheres. You should end up with around 25-30 meatballs.
- Line the baking tray with the meatballs making sure they dont touch, and bake in the oven for 20-25 mins.
- While the meatballs are baking, make the dipping sauce. In a small sauce pot, combine all the ingredients for the sauce over a medium-low heat and stir well to combine.
- Bring the sauce to a simmer for 15 mins.

How to serve:

- The meatballs and the sauce are best served warm. So if you do make the sauce ahead of time, reheat it before serving. Place the meatballs on a large serving plate, with the sauce on the side.

Chef's tips:

You can add any herbs of choice into the meatball mixture before shaping such as parsley, thyme, rosemary or oregano. Serve with pasta of your choice for a deliciously hot meatball pasta.

House Slytherin Pappardelle Pasta with Creamy Thyme Sauce

Slytherin house was always known to have a taste for the finer things in life. This is a great main dish to serve and it will please even the pickiest eaters.

Explanation: Pappardelle is a wide pasta, it will be served with a creamy coconut and thyme sauce.

Prep time: 10 mins Cook time: 30 mins Serves: 2

Materials:

- Large pot
- Medium Saucepan

Ingredients:

- 170 g (6 oz) pappardelle pasta
- 1 can coconut cream
- 4-5 sprigs of thyme
- 1 tsp onion powder
- 1 tsp garlic powder
- ¼ tsp nutmeg
- Salt and pepper to taste

Instructions:

- Bring salted water to a boil in a large pot. Boil the pasta for 10-12 minutes, depending on the brand of pasta you got, and then drain.
- While the pasta is cooking, make the sauce. In a saucepan pour the coconut cream, add the thyme, garlic powder, onion powder, nutmeg and salt and pepper. Over medium-low heat bring to a slight simmer, taste for seasoning.

- Once the pasta is cooked, put in the sauce and continue to simmer for about 2 mins, until everything is nicely incorporated.

How to serve:

- Place the pasta in the center of the plate and drizzle with olive oil and sprinkle a few thyme leaves on top. Or serve it family style with the same toppings.

Chef's tips:

Instead of drizzling olive oil, if you want to make it fancier, you can drizzle some truffle oil, it will also add incredible flavor to your dish.

Shepherd's Pie

"Harry didn't enjoy his shepherd's pie as much as he'd thought."
- Harry Potter and the Chamber of Secrets

Explanation: A hearty dish that may use up alot of leftover ingredients in the kitchen. A vegetable mixture is topped with creamy mashed potatoes and baked to get a golden brown crust.

Prep time: 30 mins Cook time: 1 hr 15 mins Serves: 4

Materials:
- Medium saucepan
- Medium pot
- Casserole dish, oven proof

Ingredients:
For the mashed potatoes
- 1 kg (2 lbs) potatoes
- 2 tbsp vegan butter
- ½ cup plant milk
- ½ tsp nutmeg

- Salt
- Pepper

For the filling

- Coconut oil, as needed
- 500 g (1 lb) vegan ground meat (1 can cooked lentils washed and strained)
- 1 small onion, diced small
- 1 medium carrot, diced small
- 2 stalks of celery, diced small
- 2 cloves garlic, minced
- 2 cups vegetable stock
- 2 tbsp vegan butter
- 1 tbsp mixed herbs, minced (tarragon, thyme, oregano)
- ¼ cup worcestershire sauce (mushroom ketchup works too)
- Salt
- Pepper

Instructions:

- Preheat the oven to 375 F. Grease your casserole dish well.
- Peel and cut the potatoes into large pieces, put into the pot and cover with salted water. Put on a high heat and boil for 15 mins or until very tender.
- Drain all the water and mash the potatoes until smooth and fluffy. Using a wooden spoon, mix in the butter, milk, nutmeg, salt and pepper. Taste for seasoning and adjust if needed. Set aside.
- Pour 2 tbsp of oil into a sauce pan, add the onions and saute for 5-8 mins. Add the carrots, celery, and garlic and continue to saute for another minute or 2. Add the vegan meat or lentils, salt pepper and herbs, mix well.
- Add the vegetable stock and simmer on low for 20 minutes, until all the vegetables are cooked and the liquid has reduced.
- Divide the mashed potatoes in half, spread half on the bottom of the casserole dish, then add the filling, then top with the rest of the mashed potatoes on top. Dot with the vegan butter and place in the oven for 30-45 minutes until the top is golden brown.

How to serve:

- After removing from the oven, cool for at least 10 minutes before serving.
- Serve in the casserole dish on the table family style.

Chef's tips:

- Using fresh herbs will always give a greater flavor to your dish.

Desserts

Mrs. Weasley's Lemon Meringue Pie

Mrs. Weasley is always making some amazing and delectable desserts for her family and guests. This recipe for lemon Meringue Pie is sure to please the fussy Weasley children.

Explanation: It is actually more of a tart, with an almost cookie-like short crust, a sweet and tart lemon curd filling, and a fluffy meringue topping.

Prep time: 30 mins Cook time: 1hr 30 mins Serves: 8

Materials:

- Pie tin (9 in.)
- Electric mixer
- Medium sized sauce pot

Ingredients:

For the dough

- 1 recipe dough (from the Cornish Pasties)

For the lemon curd

- 300 g (10.5 oz) cane sugar
- 65 g (2.5 oz) corn starch, mixed with 2 tbsp water
- ¼ tsp salt
- 235 ml (8 oz) plant milk
- 115 ml (4 oz) water
- 235 ml (8 oz) lemon juice
- Zest of 1 lemon
- 15 g (0.5 oz) vegan butter

For the meringue

- 115 ml (4 oz) Aquafaba (canned chickpea water) refrigerated
- 150 g (5 oz) powdered sugar

- ½ tsp vanilla extract
- 1 tsp lemon juice

Instructions:

- Preheat the oven to 355 F. Grease the pie tin.
- Roll out the dough into a large circle that is a ¼ in. thick and place it over the pie tin. Poke holes into the dough with a fork to prevent it from puffing up.
- Place in the oven for 20 mins, or until it starts being golden brown. Remove from the oven and set aside to cool.
- For the lemon curd, combine the sugar, salt, milk, water, lemon juice and lemon zest in a sauce pot over medium heat.
- Once the mixture starts heating up, reduce the heat to low and add the cornstarch and water mixture slowly, stirring constantly. After about 10 mins, raise the heat to medium-high while still stirring constantly for about 5-10 mins or until the mixture is thick enough to coat the back of a spoon.
- Take the sauce pot off the heat and set aside, then add in the vegan butter and whisk to incorporate. Set the mixture aside to cool completely.
- For the meringue, place the aquafaba in a large bowl and using the electric mixer, whisk on high for about 5 minutes until it starts foaming. Add the sugar, vanilla and lemon juice, then continue whisking on high again for another 10 minutes. After the meringue starts forming stiff peaks it is done.
- Place the bowl to refrigerate for at least 30 mins before assembly.
- To assemble your lovely pie, pour your cooled lemon curd into your pie crust. Then start spooning the meringue mixture on top piling it high in the center so it forms almost a meringue mountain on top of the lemon curd.

How to serve:

- Slice the lemon meringue pie into 10 equal slices for guests to enjoy. This is a great dessert for any time of year.

Chef's tips:

- Using fresh mint can be a great idea for garnish, as well as using more lemon zest sprinkled on top of the meringue.

Sherbert Lemon

Inspired by the password to dumbledore's office that was mentioned in Harry Potter and the Chamber of Secrets

Explanation: Lemon sorbet ice cream

Prep time: 10 mins Freeze time: 6 hrs Serves: 4

Materials:
- Blender
- Freezer safe container

Ingredients:
- 1 package soft tofu
- 1 cup sugar (cane sugar or agave)
- 1 cup plant milk
- ¼ cup lemon juice

Instructions:
- Put all ingredients into a blender, blend on high until everything is smooth.
- Pour into a freezer safe container and freeze for at least 6 hrs.

How to serve:
- Scoop into small bowls and enjoy on a warm day!

Chef's tips:

- Add lemon zest and fresh mint to the mixture to get that extra fresh flavor!

Treacle Pudding

"On their last evening Mrs. Weasley conjured up a sumptuous dinner that included all of Harry's favorite things, ending with a mouthwatering treacle pudding"
- Harry Potter and the Chamber of Secrets

Explanation: It is a traditional British sponge cake that is covered in an almost caramel like sauce..

Prep time: 20 mins Cook time: 1 hr Serves: 2

Materials needed:
- Small Sauce Pot
- Small Cake pan (6 in)
- Casserole dish large enough to fit the cake pan inside
- Baking paper

Ingredients:
For the cake
- 110g (4oz) Self rising Flour
- 50g (2oz) Sugar (cane sugar works best, Agave works too)
- 1 tsp baking powder
- 100 ml (4fl oz) Water (or plant milk of your choice)
- 60 ml (2.5oz) coconut oil
- 1 tbsp Golden Syrup
- ½ tsp Salt

For the treacle sauce:
- 1 cup Sugar
- ¼ cup water
- 2 ½ cup Sugar
- 1 cup boiling water
- ½ lemon, juiced

Instructions:

- Preheat the oven to 300°F
- In a medium bowl mix the flour, sugar, baking powder, and salt. Stir well to combine.
- In a small bowl stir together the water and oil. Add to the dry ingredients and whisk well together.
- Grease the cake pan well, place baking paper on the bottom and sides of the pan. Pour the batter inside the greased pan.
- Place the pan into the casserole dish, fill the dish with boiling water halfway up
- Dollop the golden syrup in several parts in the middle of the cake, it should sink to the bottom and carefully place in the oven
- Bake for 40-45 mins, until golden brown on top and when a skewer is placed through the middle of the cake and it comes out clear.
- Turn the oven off and let the cake sit inside the oven for 15 mins. (Remove the cake from the pan later while cake is still warm)
- While the cake is baking, make the treacle sauce. Take the 1 cup of sugar and mix with water in the sauce pot, turn the heat to low until the sugar dissolves. Turn the heat up to medium and caramelize the sugar, **do not stir** but make sure it doesn't burn. When the color starts getting darker, lower the heat until it is a deep brown.
- Whisk in the boiling water, carefully, then bring to a simmer. Add in the rest of the sugar and allow it to dissolve. Add the lemon juice and stir well.
- Put the heat on low and simmer for 15 mins until the sauce thickens. When thickened, set aside to cool. Take note that the sauce will continue to thicken as it cools so strain before pouring on cake if needed.

How to serve:

- Pour about ½ cup of the treacle sauce on top. Make sure both cake and sauce are warm so that the sauce will be absolved into the cake.
- Slice and serve.

Chef's tips:

- If you have a caramel sauce recipe that you like it can work instead of the treacle sauce.
- Serve with fresh berries to balance out the sweetness.

Ron's Chocolate Gâteau

Ronald Weasley is of course widely known to be a foodie, and there is nothing he loves more than desserts.

Explanation: This is a rich and chocolatey layered cake that will please at any dinner party. Gâteau = Dessert

Prep time: 20 mins Cook time: 40 mins Serves: 8

Materials needed:

- 9" cake pan
- Electric mixer
- 2 bowls

Ingredients:

For the cake

- 1 ½ cups flour
- 1 cup sugar (cane sugar works best, agave works too)
- ½ cup cocoa powder
- 1 tsp baking soda
- ½ tsp salt

- ⅓ cup vegetable oil
- 1 tsp vanilla extract
- 1 tsp white vinegar
- 1 cup water

For the chocolate cream:

- 1 ½ cups vegan butter (room temp)
- ¼ cup plant milk
- 2 tsp vanilla extract
- 1 cup cocoa powder
- 4 cups powdered sugar
- ½ cup chocolate chips
- ¼ cup almond shavings

Instructions:

- Preheat the oven to 350°F. Grease the cake pan.
- Mix together the flour, sugar, cocoa powder, baking soda, and salt.
- In a separate bowl, mix the oil, vanilla, vinegar and water.
- Combine the dry and wet ingredients, whisk well until smooth.
- Pour the batter into the cake pan and bake for 45 mins. Remove from the pan and allow to cool for 30 mins before serving
- Slice through the middle of the cake to make 2 layers and leave to cool.
- In the meantime make the buttercream. Using an electric mixer, beat the butter, milk, vanilla, cocoa powder and powdered sugar in a large bowl on high, until light and fluffy (about 8-15 mins).
- Separate ⅓ of the frosting, and fold the chocolate chips into it.
- Spread the ⅓ of the frosting on one of the layers and place the second layer on top. Use the rest of the frosting to ice the cake's top and sides. Sprinkle with almond shavings.
- Chill for at least 1 hour before serving

How to serve:

- Slice the cake into 8 equal slices, and serve on individual dessert plates

Chef's tips:

- Adding a tablespoon or 2 of espresso to the cake batter will enhance and deepen the chocolate flavor.

Golden Snitch Cake Pops

This will definitely be a party favorite at your next Harry Potter marathon.

Explanation: have fun making this portable dessert which is essentially a crumbled cake that is shaped into balls and stuck at the end of a lollipop stick, then decorated to look like the beloved and sought after golden snitch.

Prep time: 2 hrs 30 mins Cook time: 40 mins Serves: 20 cake pops

Materials:

- Lollipop sticks
- Cake pan 9 in
- Electric mixer

Ingredients:

For cake

- 1 ¾ cups flour
- 1 cup cane sugar
- 1 tsp baking soda
- ½ tsp salt
- 1 cup plant milk
- 2 tsp vanilla extract
- ⅓ cup coconut oil
- 1 tbsp apple cider vinegar

For frosting

- 3 ¾ cups powdered sugar

- 3 tbsp vegan butter at room temperature
- 4 tbsp plant milk
- 2 tsp vanilla extract

For decoration

- Golden sugar sprinkles
- 3 cups vegan white chocolate
- Gold food coloring
- 40 white chocolate wings

Instructions:

- Preheat the oven to 350 F
- Grease the cake pan well and line with baking paper
- Pour the apple vinegar into the plant milk and let it sit aside for 10 mins to slightly curdle. Mix together the flour, sugar, baking soda and salt in a bowl. In a separate bowl, mix together the milk and vinegar mixture, the vanilla and coconut oil.
- Mix the dry and wet ingredients together until smooth and no lumps remain.
- Pour cake batter into the cake pan and bake for 30 mins. After it is slightly golden on top and springs back up when touched, it is done. Set aside to cool completely.
- While the cake is cooling, make the frosting. Using an electric mixer, cream together the vegan butter, plant milk, powdered sugar and vanilla extract. Mix on high until everything is well incorporated and the frosting is pale and fluffy. This will take about 10 mins.
- Using your hands, wear rubber gloves if desired, crumble the cooled cake into a large bowl. Add the frosting to the crumbled cake ¼ cup at a time, until the cake texture is dense enough to roll into balls by hand.
- Roll out the cake mixture into balls. Each cake ball should be about 2 tbsp of the cake mixture. After all the mixture is rolled out, place on a tray and refrigerate for at least 2 hrs.
- Take the cool cake balls out of the fridge and place a lollipop stick through the top of them.
- Melt the vegan white chocolate in a microwave safe glass bowl, in intervals of 30 seconds, remove the bowl and give it a good stir until everything is smooth and melted. Pour into the chocolate a few drops of the golden food coloring and mix, add more if needed until you get a deep golden color. Pour the chocolate in a tall glass and set aside.
- Make sure the melted white chocolate in the glass is cool enough but not starting to firm up. Dip the cake pop into the chocolate until it is completely covered. Pull it out of the chocolate and sprinkle all over with the golden sugar. Do this to all the cake pops. Then when everything is cooled, stick 2 wings on each cake pop, one on each side.

How to serve:

- Make sure these cake pops are served standing to prevent any of the wings from breaking or bending. This can be done by getting a foam block and sticking the cake pops in them.

Chef's tips:

- If you do not have access to vegan white chocolate, feel free to use whatever kind of chocolate you have for the wings. But for the coating, just make a double batch of the frosting, then for the second batch, add ½ cup of plant milk to the frosting to make it easier to dip the cake pops in.

Hagrid's Rock Cakes

Hagrid was infamous for his terrible cooking, his rock cakes were described to be very dry and extremely hard to bite into. This twist on rock cakes is sure to make you come back for more.

Explanation: A vegan oatmeal raisin cookie that goes great with tea time.

Prep time: 20 mins Cook time: 20 mins Serves: 8

Materials:

- Baking tray
- Electric mixer
- Wooden Spoon

Ingredients:

- ½ cup vegan butter, room temperature
- 1 cup brown sugar (cane sugar also works)
- 1 tbsp molasses
- 1 tbsp agave
- 2 tsp vanilla extract
- 1 ½ cups oats
- 1 cup flour
- 1 tsp baking soda
- 1 tsp salt
- 1 tsp cinnamon
- ½ tsp ground nutmeg
- 2 tbsp plant milk
- ½ cup raisins

Instructions:

- Preheat the oven to 350 F. Line your tray with baking paper
- Combine the vegan butter, sugar and molasses in a bowl and mix on high for a few minutes until the mixture starts fluffing up and lightening in color. Add the agave and vanilla and cream for another 3-4 minutes.
- Add the milk, oats, flour, baking soda, salt, cinnamon and nutmeg and mix well.
- Using a wooden spoon, mix in the raisins, the dough should be thick enough to roll out by hand at this point.
- Using a tablespoon measure, measure out dough balls that are 2 tbsp each, roll them out and set them onto the baking tray. The dough should be about 1-2 in apart to make sure they don't stick together once baked.
- Place in the oven for 20 mins, then remove and set aside to cool for at least 15 minutes before enjoying to ensure the cooking has set properly.

How to serve:

- Serve on a large plate for everyone to enjoy

Chef's tips:

Go for 15 mins in the oven if you want a slightly chewier cookie.

Knickerbocker Glory

"They ate in the zoo restaurant, and when Dudley had a tantrum because his knickerbocker glory didn't have enough ice cream on top. Uncle Vernon bought him another one and Harry was allowed to finish the first." - *Harry Potter and the Sorcerer's Stone*

Explanation of Dish: A cooling ice cream sundae to enjoy on hot summer days with friends.

Prep time: 10 min / Cook time: 5 min / Serving size: 2

Materials Needed

- A tall glass and a long spoon for serving
- Ice cream scooper

Ingredients Needed

- 1 sliced banana
- 4 strawberries
- ½ cup of Blueberries
- ½ cup of Raspberries
- 1 sliced kiwi
- 2 Cherries
- 4 tbsp of raspberry syrup (or fruit syrup of choice)
- 4 tbsp of vegan chocolate syrup
- 4 scoops of vegan vanilla ice cream
- ½ cup of crushed digestive biscuits

Instructions

1. Combine banana slices, strawberries, blueberries, raspberries, kiwi slices in a bowl and set aside
2. Lightly dizzle the inside of the glass with 2 tbsp. worth of chocolate syrup from the top.
3. Begin layering your knickerbocker glory by adding roughly a ⅓ cup of fruit at the bottom followed by a scoop of ice cream.
4. Add another ⅓ cup of fruit topped with another scoop of ice cream
5. Add a light coating of crushed digestive biscuits to the ice cream
6. Drizzle 2 tbsp. worth of raspberry syrup on top
7. Place 1 cherry at the top as the final topping
8. Repeat steps 2-7 for second serving.

How to Serve

- Serve preferably in a tall glass with a tall spoon for easy access

Chef Tips

- Feel free to be as creative as you want with this recipe, adding whatever flavors and ingredients you like.

Chocolate Frogs

This popular candy was first seen in Harry Potter and the Philosopher's Stone when Harry was being introduced to many of the candies and snacks that were served on the Hogwarts Express.

Explanation: frog shaped chocolates

Prep time: 30 mins Cook time: 10 mins Serves: 8

Materials:

- Frog shaped mould
- Small pot
- Medium glass bowl

Ingredients:

- 500 g (18 oz) dark chocolate
- ⅓ cup coconut oil
- 4-5 drops orange extract

Instructions:

- Pour water halfway up the pot and put over medium heat. Once the water is heated, place the glass bowl on top of the pot, the bottom of the bowl should not touch the water, if it does you have too much water and should decrease the amount of water until it does not touch the bottom of the bowl. Put the chocolate into the bowl and stir until melted. This will take about 15 mins.
- Once the chocolate melts, add the coconut oil and orange extract and mix in well.
- Pour the chocolate mixture into the moulds and set aside to cool completely, at least 30 mins.
- Once cooled place in the fridge for another 2 hours to make sure that the chocolate has set properly.

How to serve:

- A fun way to serve this treat is to lay the chocolate frogs around the dessert section on your dinner table as if they are wanting to escape, or just on a simple platter for guests to enjoy.

Chef's tips

- You can use lavender extract, vanilla, mint or basically any other flavors you like with your chocolate instead of the orange extract.

Mrs. Weasley's English Toffee

Mrs. Weasley is no stranger to making the most delectable sweets and treats. Now we are sure hers is better but this toffee recipe is sure to make you feel at home with the Weasleys.

Explanation: A caramel topped with nuts and chocolate cut into square shaped pieces for you to easily enjoy.

Prep time: 20 mins Cook time: 30 mins Serves: 30 squares

Materials:

- Medium pot
- Candy thermometer
- 1-2 baking trays

Ingredients:

- 2 cups vegan butter, room temperature
- 2 ½ cups sugar (white or cane sugar)
- 1 tbsp maple syrup
- 1 cup plant milk
- 1 tsp salt
- 1 cup nuts of your choice (cashews and pecans work best)
- 300 g (10.5 oz) dark chocolate

Instructions:

- Grease the baking trays well and line with baking paper.
- Place the chocolate in a microwave safe glass bowl and melt the chocolate. It should take from 5-8 minutes, make sure to take the bowl out every 30 secs- 1 minute to stir so everything can melt properly. When melted, Set aside while warm
- Lightly crush the nuts and set aside.
- In the pot add the butter, sugar, maple syrup, milk and salt onto a medium/high heat. Stir to mix everything until all the sugar melts properly. Add in the sugar thermometer standing up at the side of your pot and continue stirring. Once the thermometer reads 285 F, quickly but carefully pour onto the baking trays. You can use a silicone spoon to spread it out to make sure it is all even.
- Sprinkle your nuts over the hot toffee evenly. Then pour the chocolate over the toffee and nuts and smooth it out so that it covers all the toffee and nuts.
- Place the tray in the fridge for at least 2 hours, then cut the toffee with a knife into medium sized squares.

How to serve:
- Serve on a platter for guests to easily enjoy

Chef's tip:
- You can add some coarsely crushed nuts on top of the chocolate before it sets.
- You can add your favorite type of dried fruit to the mix as well for garnish.

Queenie's Apple Strudel

"Queenie: Hey Mr. Scamander, you prefer pie or strudel?
Newt: I really don't have a preference.
Queenie (looking at Jacob): You prefer strudel, huh honey?
Strudel it is."
-Fantastic Beasts and Where to Find Them

Explanation: It is originally an Austrian dessert or a popular tea accompaniment. It is a layered and flaky dough that has a sweet filling, most often apple.

Prep time: 45 mins Cook time: 30 mins Serves: 5

Materials needed:
- Small Sauce Pot
- Small pan
- Oven Proof tray
- Parchment paper

Ingredients:
- ¼ cup of raisins
- 3 tbsp apple brandy (apple cider)
- 1 tbsp vegan butter
- 1 tbsp coconut oil
- ⅓ cup breadcrumbs
- ⅓ cup raw cane sugar (agave can work too)
- ½ tsp salt
- 1 tsp cinnamon
- ½ tsp nutmeg powder
- ½ tsp ginger powder
- ½ tsp cloves powder

- 1 tbsp lemon juice
- 4 Gela Apples (peeled)
- ½ cup simple syrup (½ cup water + 4 tbsp sugar)
- Vegan puff pastry dough
- Flour
- Powdered sugar to serve

Instructions:

- Thaw the puff pastry dough if frozen. Preheat the oven to 400°F. Grease a baking tray and line with parchment paper.
- In a small sauce pot, pour the apple cider and raisins and bring the fire to a medium-low heat. When it comes to a simmer, cover and then set aside allowing the raisins to absorb the liquid.
- Place the butter on the pan over medium heat. Once the butter melts, sprinkle the bread crumbs and shake them around. Toast them until golden brown (it should take about 5-7 mins).
- Cut the apples into small cubes and place in a bowl with the raisins, breadcrumbs, salt, sugar, lemon juice, cinnamon, nutmeg, ginger, and cloves. Stir to combine well and set aside.
- Flour the surface you are working on and roll out the puff pastry dough to a 12"x14" rectangle
- Pour the apple mixture along the width of the center of the pastry. Brush water on the edges and fold over so that the edges meet. Crump the edges down with a fork to make sure it is sealed well.
- Brush the top with coconut oil and sprinkle with some cane sugar. Make small incisions down the length of the top of the dough to allow the air to escape.
- Bake in the oven for 20-25 mins, or until golden brown.

How to serve:

- This is best eaten warm. When it is out of the oven, sprinkle the top with powdered sugar, slice, and serve.

Chef's tips:

- Though it is possible to make it at home, make your life easier by buying ready made vegan puff pastry dough. It is a long and tedious process to make your own at home.

We hope you were able to appreciate and enjoy the fantastical world of Harry Potter in a whole new, delicious way. We hope that every bite of every meal you made, allowed you to feel just like you were in the books with Harry and his friends each time you closed your eyes.

Fiction is such a beautiful way in which we can explore our imagination. There's a magical spark we get from reading good stories, watching good stories – produced as a television show or film.

Now, thanks to this book, you can immerse yourself even further within your favorite fictional works, through food!

We hope you had as much fun making and tasting these drinks as we did! Be sure to check out our *Harry Potter Cocktails and Mocktails* for delicious drinks (vegan-friendly) you can pair with the meals from this book, for an even more accurate Harry Potter world experience!

Printed in Poland
by Amazon Fulfillment
Poland Sp. z o.o., Wrocław

66184576R00043